ISBN: 979-8-9896484-0-5

Come to Me
Called the Sea

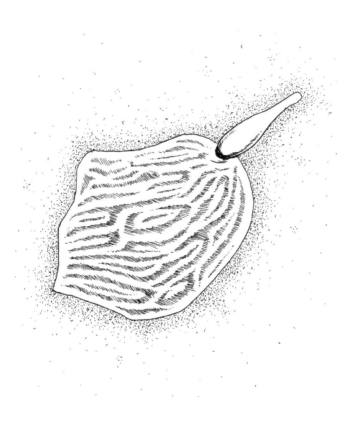

Written by Maria Best

Illustrated & designed by Al Best

To the Lightworkers

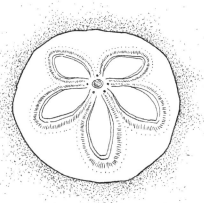

At the shore you will find a door
       where there only is and there is no more.

"Climb out of the sun

and step into the fog,"

said the salty ol' sailor
with a blue-eyed dog.

"I was once was
and forever will be,

take off your shoes

and splash with me."

"Float like the fish

you beings
of land,

ride the white current,

put your toes in the sand."

I spotted a ninja all dressed in black

collecting sea treasures

and giving them back.

"Sit and be still," the sea shore said,

so I perched
with a bird

while he gobbled his bread.

I followed his prints,

his feet were so small,

his feathers escaped him like leaves in the fall.

The sand dollar broke open
her time was complete,

releasing her doves
to offer a treat.

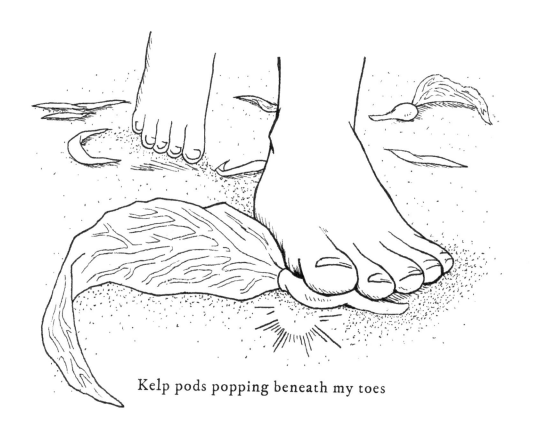

Kelp pods popping beneath my toes

inviting the joy
and crunching the woes.

The tide turned the sand into a tree

then disappeared rejoining the sea.

Sandpipers scurrying

back
    and
        forth

being brave,

taking turns leading while chasing a wave.

The sun's reflection now burning bright,

my shadow dancing with delight.

Two horses strode by
    one rider was humming,
        gave a nod as they passed
            and left my heart strumming.

Sand crabs digging—

going where I don't know,

somewhere more quiet

and away from the glow.

Otter said,

"Shhhhh, let the tide set the pace.

No need to rush, this isn't a race."

Waves splashed goodbye whispering,
"Please come back soon.
Next time you visit,

let's invite the moon."

For anyone passing seeking to find,
an abundance of peace,

love and laughter
were all that was left behind.

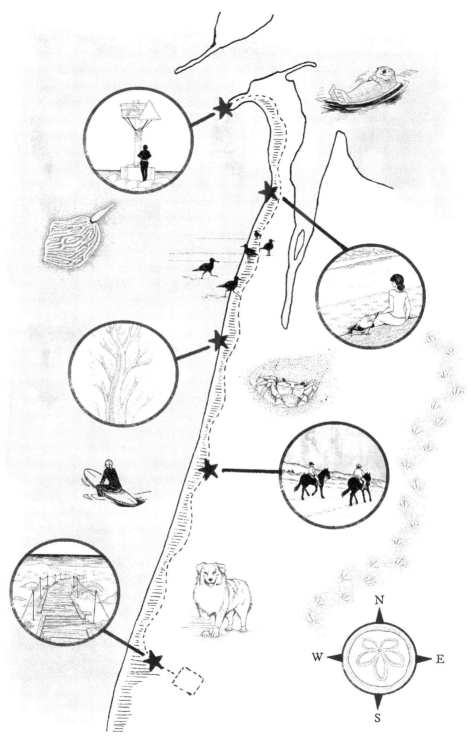

Moss Landing

One of thirteen national marine sanctuaries in the
United States, the Monterey Bay National Marine
Sanctuary covers 5,312 square miles, one and a
half times the size of the largest national park in
the continental U.S. At its center is an underwater
canyon twice as deep as the Grand Canyon.

Monterey Canyon, one of the largest
submarine canyons in North America, begins
in Moss Landing.

The underwater cliffs, gorges, valleys, and kelp
forests provide a diverse habitat, home, and nursery
to one of the most unique and abundant marine
ecosystems on our planet.